BenWicks'
WOMEN

Ben Wicks
Oct 1978

"Woman may be said to
be an inferior man."
Aristotle,
fourth century, B.C.

"I expect that woman will
be the last thing civilized
by man."
George Meredith, 1859.

BEN WICKS' WOMEN

by Ben Wicks

McClelland and Stewart

To Doreen, Susan, Kim,
and me Mum . . .
the women in my life.

The Canadian Publishers
McClelland and Stewart Limited
25 Hollinger Road
Toronto, Ontario
M4B 3G2

Canadian Cataloguing in Publication Data

Wicks, Ben, 1926–
  Ben Wicks' women

ISBN 0-7710-8982-1

1. Women – Caricatures and cartoons. I. Title.

NC1763.W6W53   741.5'971   C78-001320-4

Printed and bound in the United States of America

Acknowledgments

This book could not have been written
without the help of a number of people.
All women.
Although the deft hand of man was
needed to put the material together,
I am indebted to my editor, Joan Kerr,
and the staff of women under the
leadership of Anna Porter at
McClelland and Stewart.

CREDITS

Grateful acknowledgement is made to the following for photographs:

p. 11, *Nothing Sacred*, Hal Roach; p. 12, *A Small Town Girl*, (1917); p. 19, Stan Wayman, Life Magazine, © 1965, Time Inc.; p. 20, Burt Glinn, Rex Features Limited; p. 26, *Shadows of Paris*; p. 27, *King Kong* (1933) RKO; p. 38, *Ten Commandments*, (1923); p. 39, *The Sheik*, (1921); p. 42, *Man's Genesis*, (1912); p. 45, *Cleopatra* copyright © 1963 Twentieth Century Fox Productions, Ltd. All rights reserved; p. 47, *I Am a Fugitive from a Chain Gang*, (1932) Warner Bros.; p. 49, *Manslaughter*, (1922); p. 54, Acme; p. 59, Museum of Modern Art; p. 60, Bill Eppridge, Life Magazine © 1969, Time Inc.; p. 60, Fred P. Peel; p. 66, Doug Griffin; pp. 96-99, John Muller; p. 103, *Manslaughter*, (1922); p. 104, *The Sheik*, (1921); p. 109, *The Lost World*, (1925); p. 115, *The Vanishing American*; p. 116, *Mockery*, (1927); p. 117, Museum of Modern Art; p. 121, Lothrop Withington, United Press International; p. 122, *Ten Commandments*, (1923); p. 123, *Barbed Wire*; p. 126, *What Price Glory?*; p. 138, *The Mysteries of Myra*, (1916); p. 142, *The Intrigue*, (1916); p. 143, *Laugh, Clown, Laugh*, (1928); p. 153, Associated Press Photo; p. 160, Nina Leen, Life Magazine, © 1947, Time Inc.

Contents

God's Biggest Blunder

In the beginning there was man.
Then there was woman.
Why would God, having created the
perfect being the first time around,
try again and mess up the mould?
No-one knows.
The fact is, he did.
Conscious of God's original request that he rule the earth,
man struggles bravely to carry out God's wishes,
despite the handicap of his having such an inferior partner.

Woman, unaware of her shortcomings, continues
to look on as man shoulders his burdens.
But surely enough is enough!
Man is exhausted.
He deserves, nay *must*
get a crack at living
the good life.
It's time that woman left her life of ease
and placed her shoulder to the wheel.

Today's woman wants to emulate man. . . . Let her!

Let her tote that barge.
Let her lift that bale.
Let her get a little drunk
and land in jail.

But is she capable?
A close study is required to answer that one.
What does she do during the day?
What does she do during the night?
What does she do, period?
Where did she come from, and where is she at?

PART ONE

Woman's Problem?

Boredom.
woman is bored with her
role of homemaker and is
looking for ways to escape
from her happy-go-lucky
life of ease.
Although frustrated that
she is unable to gain
ground with man, she presses
on regardless.
Haunted by the knowledge
that her intellect does
not equip her to compete
in a man's world, woman
blames man for her failings.

*Bored out of her
skull, a typical
housewife waits to
give her husband
hell for arriving
home on time.*

But the fault is neither man's nor woman's.

Woman: What Is It?

Looks somewhat different to man.
Has a high-pitched voice.
Lives on a steady diet of birth-
control pills.
"Never has a thing to wear."
Is "never ever taken anywhere."
And gets bored staying inside
the house that she had always
dreamed of owning.

In short . . .
a disaster!
Surely God's greatest disappointment.
"What man needs is someone to give
him a bit of 'love and cherish,' "
said God in the beginning.

What man got was an army of screamers
anxious to take on the role of leader.

Unable to recognize the benefits of
being a servant to man, woman has
decided that she needs a change of role.

But is woman capable of changing?

Let's face it.
Women have always been slower both mentally
and physically than men.
Yet surprisingly the brain of a woman
is the same size as that of a man.

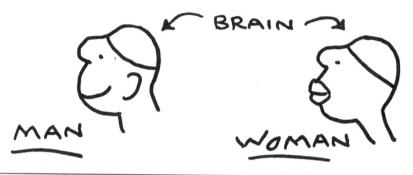

The author with a man.

The author with a woman.

Why is it that woman is
less intelligent than
man?
For the simple reason
that with man around
to do the thinking
for her, woman has
had little need
for intellect.

This lack of activity by the brain has caused it to stagnate.

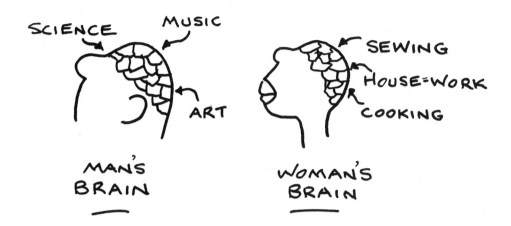

This is not to minimize the efforts of the many women throughout history who have assisted men in many areas, for example:

Whistler's mother who filled in so readily when
a model failed to show up for a sitting.

It was a woman who
helped the great French
scientist Curie with
his many experiments.

And it was Eliza Dolittle who worked her fingers
to the bone selling flowers (despite her name)
and helped make Professor Higgins a household name.

I mention these facts at the beginning of the book to
show that, far from being prejudiced, I am being more
than fair in acknowledging the outstanding contributions
that women have made in the world of man.

Surely such contributions are enough to keep women in their kitchens, whistling.

Not so.

WATCH THAT CLOUD!

These tastes of man's world have only helped to increase woman's desire to get out and poke her nose into man's territory.

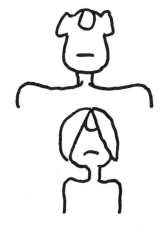

Fortunately for exhausted man, women everywhere are pushing and shoving in a crazed attempt to take the responsibility of running the world from his wise and dependable shoulders.

Woman:
The Beginning

FAIR HAIR

BLUE EYES

GENTLE HANDS

ADAM

Woman was made from the rib of a man named Adam.
It happened this way.
Having finished heaven and earth in six days, God sat down on a brand new rock and dangled his feet in a brand new babbling brook.
"What I need now is someone to admire my work," he said to no-one.
He lifted his hand and flicked his fingers.
A butterfly opened its wings toward the sun and floated away.
God began to giggle.
"This is fun," he thought as he began a rat-a-tat-tat of flicking fingers.

Animals and birds flew from his hands
with the speed of baked beans dropping
down the throat of a hungry cowboy.
Flick ... a Brontosaurus.
Flick ... a Pterodactyl.
Flick ... a Spider.
Pursing his lips, God began to whistle.
He got up and started to wade along the stream.
Fish and flies, cockroaches and bees,
followed in his wake.
Life had arrived on earth and God was in his glory.

Still all was not right.
Sure the creatures
were great and small,
but what of their
conversation?
Nil!
Nothing but

You'll never guess who just got D.D.T'D!

WOW

where the next meal was coming from and whose hind
legs were fastest when
rubbed together.
God gathered up a
handful of dust.
"What I need is someone
like me, someone who's
interested in the same
things as me."
He threw some dust at
the nearest bush and there
in the middle of the leaves
stood a man.

And what a man!
Perfect in every way.

God tickles a brand new kitten.

God and Adam
quickly became friends.
Knowing Adam's interest
in gardening, God soon
made a plot of land
appear and handed
a shovel and tools
to Adam.

"I've had a very busy week," said God, "and I want
you to do something for me, Adam.
I'm going off to get a little sleep.
Take care of things while I'm gone."

It's as well to stop at this point and reflect on
what God was implying. He was telling Adam that he,

man, is second-in-command under the big chief.
I mention this in passing.

"Just one thing, Adam," said God.

"Do not touch that tree there.

The one with the apples."

"What's so special about that tree?" asked Adam.

"That tree is the tree of knowledge, good and evil,"
replied God. "Touch that tree and you'll be back
in the dirt again
in less time than it
takes to cut your
toe-nails."

"It's going
to be tough
taking care of things
all by
myself,"
said Adam.
"How be
I give you
someone to help?" God offered.

"Mate or man?" asked Adam grinning.

"Mate," said God.

"That's more like it," said Adam. God glared. Being all-knowing he had recognised that man was anxious for hanky-panky.
"In no way have I worked this hard," thought God "just to have some hot-to-trot guy ruin the whole development."

MAN ANXIOUS FOR HANKY-PANKY

Staring into Adam's eyes, God began to speak in a low voice.
"You are going to sleep," said God, "sleep . . . sleep . . . sleep. . . ."
Adams eyelids fell with a plop and his head sank to his chest.

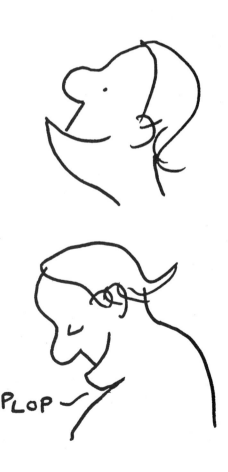

PLOP

"Now what?" thought God. "If I don't bring a mate for Adam, **he**'ll be getting into trouble – and if I do bring a mate for Adam, he'll be

ADAM, ONE
REST, TWO

getting **her** into trouble."
The day wore on as God grappled with the problem.
Obviously something drastic had to be done.
Adam must be fixed!
"Part of his body must be removed to slow him down," thought God.
"His head? No!"
"His legs? No!"
"His arms? No!"
"A rib? That's it!
A rib. I'll take a rib.
Better than that.
I'll use the rib to make Adam's mate."

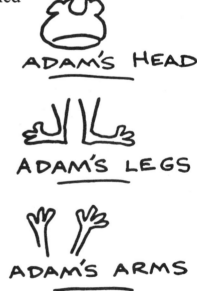

ADAM'S HEAD

ADAM'S LEGS

ADAM'S ARMS

24

God began to chortle, then quickly stopped
fearing that he would wake Adam.
He reached over
Adam's sleeping
body and lifted
his right arm
above his head.
Then carefully

he moved his index finger down Adam's side and
reached into the opening he had made.
The rib came away with a loud crack.
God held his breath.
Adam was still sleeping.
God heaved a sigh of relief
then quickly nipped behind
a large tree and got to work.

It was a long tough night....
Making a woman out of a
rib is not exactly a
pushover.

FOLD
ALONG
DOTTED
LINE

The sun was already on the rise
as God with a final sigh pushed
the last piece of rib into place.
She was gorgeous, there's no
doubt about that.
Long legs, big eyes and
a great figure.

*There are no known photographs of Eve. However,
evidence seems to point to her looking something like the
woman in the above picture. Since Eve was without
clothes, a certain amount of imagination is called for.*

"Here! What's going on?"
Her high-pitched voice clawed the air.
"What have I done?" thought God.
"She may be a cracker, but her voice
has sure slipped a few gears."
"Here you! I'm talking to you!"
Her voice hit God around the head
forcing him to cover his ears.

A flirty Eve watches from the safety of a tree-top as two of God's newest creatures battle for her affections.

"Who me?" he asked.
"Well, I ain't exactly talking to the trees, mate. Now what's all this about and where am I?"
"You're in the garden of Eden," replied God. "And I suppose you're Eden," Eve cut in. "You don't understand. I've just made you."
"Out of what? Old rope?" the woman giggled.
"Er no, Adam's rib," replied God.

WANNA MESS AROUND?

READY OR NOT, BOYS – HERE I COME!

"You feeling all right, Grandad?"
"Yes thank you," replied God.
"Well, I'll tell you what," said Eve, "you go and have a little shut-eye, while I wander around this little cabbage patch and find myself something nearer my own age."

She pushed herself roughly past God
and vanished from view.
Puzzled and tired, God lay down.
"I'll worry about her in the
morning," he thought as he
turned on his side and
quickly fell asleep.

The Meeting

The soft, damp grass glistened
in the morning sunlight as
Adam made his way toward a berry
bush at the end of the garden.
His long deep sleep had
made him hungry.
Reaching out, he took a small
firm berry in his fingers and
pulled.
"Here! Hold on! What do you think
you're doing?"
Adam recoiled in horror.
Eve stood rubbing her nipple.
"Who are YOU?" cried Adam
in amazement.
"Someone who doesn't like being
mauled, that's who!"
"I'm sorry," spluttered Adam.
"I was looking for berries."
"Well I'm sorry to disappoint
you, but these are Eve's."
"You don't understand.
These are berries," said Adam
pointing to the berries on the bush.

BERRY

BERRY
BUSH

BERRY

EVE

"Well, next time watch where you're picking,"
smiled Eve, who by now had noticed that Adam
was the best looker she had seen all day.
"Are you a girl?" asked Adam.
"Well, I ain't a donkey,"
answered Eve.
"Sorry," said Adam. "But
you see, I've never seen
a girl before."
"That's all right. You're
only the second man I've
seen. I'm Eve. Who are you?"
"I'm Adam. Happy to meet you."
Both stood looking each other up and down.
"Want to go for a walk?" asked Eve.
"Where to?" asked Adam.

— HI
THERE!

"How about down to the
lily pond?"
Before Adam could reply
an awful, slimy, greasy
voice rang out.
"Hi there me beauties."
A serpent slithered from
beneath a rock and
settled on Eve's foot.

"Come on, Eve," said Adam. Let's go and pick berries
and leave this rude thing to go about his business."
The serpent suddenly rolled over and roared with laughter.

"Pick berries . . . pick berries! You can't
be serious. You're going to
pick berries with
a tree just twenty
yards away laden with
ripe, red apples?"
"It may interest you
to know," said Adam
"that God has forbidden
us to eat the fruit
from that tree."

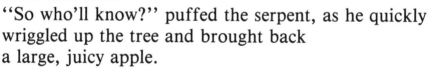

"So who'll know?" puffed the serpent, as he quickly
wriggled up the tree and brought back
a large, juicy apple.
"Here, Eve. Have a bite!"
Eve stepped back in horror.
"Not me!"
"Chicken!"
said the
snake.
"Oh yea?"
said Eve
and quickly
snatched the
apple.

"You sure it's okay, Serp?"
"You have my word," said the snake.
Eve took a large bite.
"Now you've done it!"
screamed the snake,
wriggling with delight.
"What are you getting at,
greasy legs?" snarled Eve.

The serpent quickly changed his tune.
"Okay . . . okay . . . it's nothing. Let's
be friends. Let me introduce myself.
I'm serpent."
Still uncertain,
Eve replied coldly. "I'm Eve,
and this piece of jelly behind
me is Adam."
The serpent began to snicker.
"What's so funny?" asked Eve,
ready to put her foot in the snake's mouth.
"Well I can't help noticing that you
and Adam are not wearing any clothes,"
chortled the snake.
"Who needs clothes?" asked Adam
easing his way from behind Eve.
"You do," said the snake,
"Look at you both. You've
got your private parts hanging
out all over the place."
"Take no notice," said Eve,
"he's just jealous because
we've got more legs than he has."

HAS
HE
GONE?

ONLY ONE?

"Now you're for it!" laughed the snake
as he hurried off through the grass.

Adam and Eve looked on in amazement.

"Could it be their bodies he
was laughing at?" thought Adam.
"That must be it!"

Adam turned to Eve.
"Quick, grab this."
Adam handed Eve a leaf.

"What do you want me
to do with this?" she asked.

"Hide yourself."

"What are you? Some
kind of a nut?" answered
Eve holding up the small
leaf between two fingers.

EVE AND
LEAF
(TO SCALE)

"Not all of you,"
answered Adam. "Just your naughty bit."

Adam quickly pointed to the area in question
as he covered his own vital parts.

"Hello, hello, hello." A loud booming
voice rang out across the garden.

Adam turned.

"Well, well, well,"
he said in as
friendly a voice
as he could
muster, "if it
isn't God."

Eve gave a
nervous giggle
and ran forward.
"How are you,
Grandad?
Nice to see you,
I'm sure," said Eve
giving God's arm a little squeeze.

"Don't give me all that soft stuff," roared God as he
threw off her arm.
"What's with the leaves?"
"What leaves?" asked Adam.
"Those leaves at the tops of your legs."
"Where?" asked Eve turning to hide her cover.
"There!" said God leaning forward and pointing.

"Oh these leaves?" said
Eve turning.
"They're just a little
something we threw together.
Like them?"
"Like them?" rasped God.
"Why you pair of good-for-nothing
nincompoops. I told you no covers.
No clothes. Savvy?"
God pushed his face into Eve's.
He suddenly stopped and,
lifting his head, sniffed the air.
"What's that smell?"
"Er, berries?" asked Eve nervously.
"Berries my eye!
That's apple I can smell."
He lept into the air and boomed

**"YOU'VE BEEN AT THE TREE
OF KNOWLEDGE."**

Eve and Adam cowered beneath his fury.

"**HE** made me do it!" screamed Eve pointing
at Adam who by now was attempting to get
behind her again.
"That's a lie," cried Adam. "It was her.
She made me try a bite."
"No . . . no. . . . It was the snake.
That one over there hiding
under that rock," shouted Eve.
"Me?" shouted the snake.
"I've never seen them before
in my life."
Suddenly all three were shouting
and blaming each other.

"Quiet!" thundered God.
"You're all guilty and you're all
going to get what's coming to you.
"You, serpent, will crawl around on your
stomach in the dirt for the rest of your natural life
and on into eternity. And you," said God raising himself
above the cringing Eve, "you will have
children and each delivery will be a
painful one. And as for you, Adam."
God turned to face the cowering being.
"You will work like a dog all your life
and end your days by returning to the
dust from whence you came."

"Now line up, all of you.
Tallest on the right
shortest on the left."
The three unhappy
creatures did as
they were told.
"Put these on,"
said God hopelessly
as he threw Adam
and Eve a set of clothes.

"Now GET OUT!" he commanded pointing to the
exit sign at the end of the garden.
Adam and Eve lowered their eyes and slowly left
the garden as the snake slithered toward the
dirt and dust of the outside world.

The sky was suddenly
dark and thunder
rolled across the land,
as earth's first woman
took the hand of the
kind and gentle Adam
and slowly led him
toward the cold and
distant hills.

OUT!

WE
FORGOT
TO SAY
GOODBYE!

*Dressed in their new clothes, Adam instructs Eve
not to turn around as they leave the Garden of Eden.*

Women: Through the Ages

The Stone Age

Woman's first home was a cave.
The cave had walls.
Walls equalled boredom.
Hour after hour
woman looked
at walls.

There had to be an answer.
Woman found it.
Man would paint the walls.
Although tired and exhausted after a hard day
of hunting, man slapped the wet stuff around
the cave. Horses, dragons, sheep. All thrown
up against the wall as man tried his best to
satisfy his incredibly bored mate.

Forced to work in the dark, many men were never exactly sure who the creature was in the corner.

If the results found on cave walls today are, as many experts feel, drawings of man's mate, then woman has indeed come a long way.

YOUNG GIRL

ELDERLY WOMAN

41

So time passed.
Caves gave way to huts.
Raw meat gave way
to cooked meat.

Woman gave way
to her children.
The tiny feet
demanded all
her attention.

No longer was
she able to
supply man
with his basic
requirement.

Although she has killed a defenseless man, an early woman is comforted by her husband. He has taken the axe from her and stands ready to take the blame as two detectives arrive on the scene.

A PENNY FOR YOUR THOUGHTS!

A set of excuses was
quickly devised.
"We'll wake the children."
"The neighbours will hear."
"Have you been drinking again?"
And the most popular excuse
of them all . . .
"Is that **all** you ever think
about?"

Man grew restless.
Woman grew worried.
"Is he having his basic needs fulfilled elsewhere?"

DO YOU TAKE THIS WOMAN?

What woman needed was another set of rules.
She found them on a licence called "marriage."

Ancient Egypt

"Make man so busy that he'll
never notice what we're doing."
This was the cry of the women
of ancient Egypt.
Sneaking behind the throne of Kings,
woman sowed her seed.
"If you want to get to heaven
there's only one way to go,"
she whispered.
"Get buried under a pile of old rocks
built in the shape of a triangle."
"And who will build these pyramids?"
asked the Kings.
"The men of course,"
answered the women.
"And who will make them?"
asked the Kings
"Other men, of course."
"And where will the women be?"
"Floating down the Nile on golden barges."
"And who will be rowing them?"
asked the Kings.
"Who else?"

Having enjoyed a slide with her child a woman of ancient Egypt walks smugly past the exhausted park keepers.

Ancient Greece

The constant mention of the words,
"Not tonight dear, I have a headache,"
began to leave their mark.
Man turned to man
for his affection.
Furious at this
outcome, woman
fought to lure
man back to his
original interests.
Man would have none of it.

Incredibly jealous, woman formed into large
armies led by a gal by the name of Helen,
out of Troy, and thousands of the sex-starved beasts
set out to hunt man down.

Desperate to
escape, man
fled to the
woods and
once there
began to
grow a

number of disguises.
Ears, horns, and extra legs.
All was to no avail.
One by one they were dragged from their hiding places
by Helen and her hench-women, and returned
to town in a large wooden horse. Then they were
ravished and pillaged throughout the long nights.

Once again, woman had
what she wanted.
But it was to man that she
looked for an "advance."

Ancient Rome

Woman had slowly regained
her pre-Greek hold on man.
With the help of peek-a-boo
clothes, woman successfully
steered man's
attention away
from man; and soon reminded
him that woman was his
official opposite partner.
For many men the sudden
change was traumatic.
Long sleepless nights with
one of each sex caused
their hair to recede.
"So who ever said hair
looked great?" asked
anxious women as they
quickly slapped bunches
of dead leaves on every
bald spot in sight.
With dead leaves for hair,
and some dressed in
short skirts while others
wore long dresses,
man looked ridiculous.

Ever anxious to please,
man had become a clown!
Ever anxious to be kind,
man had become a fool.
Ever anxious to be gentle,
man had jumped through a hoop.
And who was holding the hoop?   Who else?

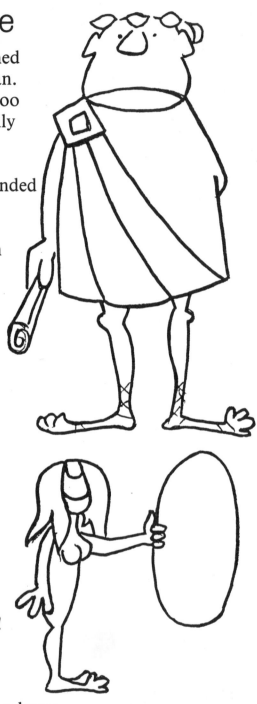

49

The Dark Ages

"Lights out! Time to sleep!" Puff!
She leaned across her man and blew out the candle.

Woman by this simple action had forced the world into it's most sorrowful hour.
No light.
No reading.
No writing.
No learning.
No discoveries.
Man had been forced to stand still . . . and with man, the world. Earth was in the dark and woman was once again out in the cold.

Oscar winning movie star, Shirley Jones listens in utter disbelief as the immensely likable author describes the plight of woman in the dark ages.

The Middle Ages

A time when knights were bold and rescued
women in distress. Though many women claim
that if it hadn't been for men, they wouldn't
have been in distress in the first place.
Nonsense.
Knights were gentlemen.
They were constantly galloping off to
rescue a maiden from a dragon.
Snatching her from the jaws of danger,
the knights would ride back to their
castles. Their drawbridge would go up
and once their drawbridge had gone
down once more, the maiden was
quickly released.

KNIGHT
(DRAWBRIDGE UP)

Seventeenth-Eighteenth Century

The whip.
Man's greatest friend
had arrived.
Woman would do man's
bidding once more. . . .
Not true.
Woman began to enjoy
the feel of the lash!
"More, more, more,"
she cried as,
puzzled and exhausted,
man lifted his arm
time and time again
in order to satisfy
his mate's new craving.
Masochism over sadism.
Poor de Sade.
Once the hero of
man.
The finder of a new
weapon and a new word.
Sadism was in and
de Sade was out.

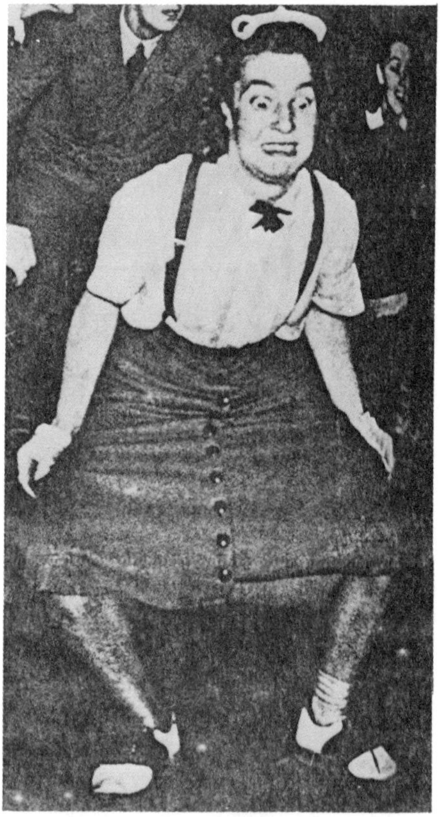

*Mrs Wilmer Jenkins seen here
soon after her husband had
given her a de Sade whip
for her birthday.
One stroke for each year.*

Out to lunch in more ways than one.
For de Sade ended his life in an insane asylum.

The Industrial Revolution

Woman wanted more.
More dresses.
More shoes.
More hats.
More of everything.

Man wanted more.
More help to make the things that woman wanted.

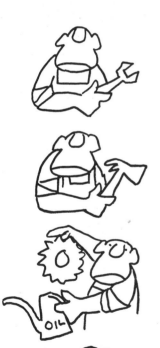

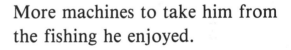
More industry to take him from
the farming that he loved.

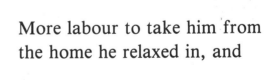
More machines to take him from
the fishing he enjoyed.

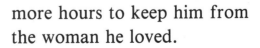
More labour to take him from
the home he relaxed in, and

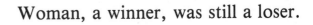
more hours to keep him from
the woman he loved.

Woman, a winner, was still a loser.

Woman: Today

Inspired by the successful publicity antics
of the suffragette, woman has lept into the
twentieth century shoes of man with both feet.
Woman has firmly reached for
the first rung of a ladder
that she feels will lead her
to equality and happiness.
Nurses want to
become doctors.
Secretaries want to
become executives.
Stewardesses want to
become pilots.

But can they handle it?
It's doubtful.

Where the heil is Eva?

Nurses

Frustrated doctors.
Usually found behind glassed-in rooms reading . . . as buzzers sound everywhere.
Dorothy Parker best summed up the profession when she related her brief stay in hospital.
On being visited by a friend, Parker reached for the button that would summon the nurse.
"Why did you press that?" asked the friend.
"I want to ensure that we have 45 minutes of uninterrupted conversation," answered Parker.

Women Doctors

As above without caps.

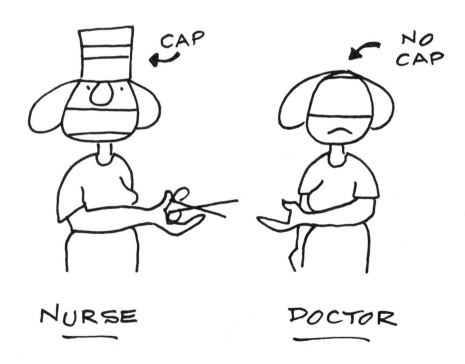

CAP

NO CAP

NURSE   DOCTOR

Secretaries

Excellent coffee-makers and servants.

Given grand titles (i.e. Executive) when required by men to work longer hours for the same pay.

Office Workers

As above with less pay.

Women Executives

A rare breed.

Knowing the secret of man's needs, most have supplied these . . . and now find themselves behind a large desk empty of the essential – a group of family pictures.

Stewardesses

In-air housewives.
Dressed in
sexy uniform.
Purpose:
to encourage
predominantly
male travellers to
forget how late the
plane will be in reaching
its destination, and so
avoid ugly letters to the
president.

David Niven is obviously impressed by the brilliant Wicks as the modest author describes his plan for women.

Waitresses

By far the job most suited to women.
Able to work long hours serving food
to hungry men, most waitresses are
content beyond belief.
Extra delights:
Huge amounts of money left by
generous men under each plate.

Cleaning Women

The truly dedicated women.
Salt of the earth.
Free of ambition, she scrubs
and slaves, happy that the
foot of man walks on her clean
and shining floor.

Woman: Entertainment

Stage

Of all the areas woman has poked her unwanted nose into, surely entertainment is the most unsuitable. Nightly, money-paying audiences throughout the world suffer embarrassment and discomfort as female troupers invade a territory that so obviously belongs to man.

Ingrid Bergman remains unpersuaded as the incredibly modest author explains why he would have been more convincing playing the female lead in the movie "Casablanca."

THIS IS FUN !

It was not always this way. From the time of the Greek Theatre and on through the Renaissance period, no woman had ever dared to set foot on the stage of man. (Unless to clean it.) All women were much too happy up to their knees in a babbling brook banging their husbands' dirty shirts against the largest and roundest rock available.

Film

"Half-dressed female-squeaking forms
flittered across the screen and pushed
their wet and sticky, lipstick covered lips
across the mouths of
English-speaking
heroes who were about to utter,
in round, perfect tones,
words that caused the spine
to quiver,"
wrote an early film critic.

Ballet

Audiences the world over pay good money to see men dance. What do they see when they get to the theatre? A woman constantly in his way.

Man is forced to spend the evening picking her up and placing her down again well outside the dancing area.

MAN   MAN   MAN + WOMAN

This wonderful before and after photograph clearly shows how well man can dance once a partner has been persuaded that the world of ballet is no place for a woman.

Is it any wonder that ten minutes of this picking up,
lifting and twisting, leaves the dancing man with
little to offer but a sweat-covered body?

And the woman?
Rested after being carried around
the stage, she is able to leap,
prance, and stand on her toes.
Nothing but a huge bunch of
flowers is able to hold her
down.

Sport

Nowhere in the world of entertainment is woman better reminded that she does not belong, than in the world of sport. Here her frailties and weaknesses are finally brought into the open. Determined to attract attention, she skates, runs, jumps, throws, skis, pole-vaults, and swims her way into record books – knowing that at any time man can surpass her achievements.

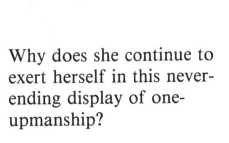

Why does she continue to exert herself in this never-ending display of one-upmanship?

The shrewd and impartial author tells tennis star, Bobby Riggs, that his defeat by Billie Jean King was pure bad luck.

Faced with these facts, it is my sincere hope that woman will quickly switch her talents to where they are so obviously needed: Coal-mining, steel mills, sweeping streets, and car assembly.

If woman wants to be equal, surely these are the areas to tackle.

Let's face it . . . certain areas are better left to man.

Jobs that man alone can handle. After all, short of giving birth, man is capable of anything.

Unfortunately, woman is not.

PART TWO

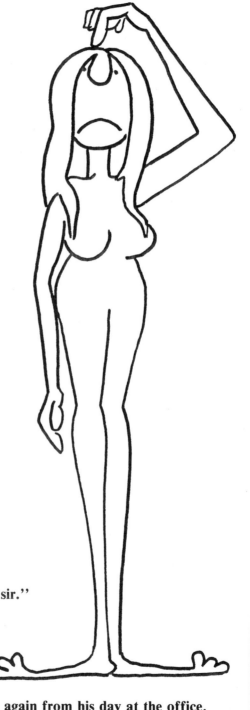

At the Crossroads

Woman is at a cross-road.
One leads to equality
and the other to supremacy.

Which should she take?

Neither.

The road to happiness for
woman lies back the way
she has come.

Back to those carefree
days of subservience.

Back to her days of "yes sir, no sir."

Back to the simple life of
give and give.
A life of ease broken only
by the sounds of the
long-awaited footsteps of her
happy partner as he returns once again from his day at the office.
Luckily for exhausted man, woman is looking ahead – not back.

Donny Osmond speaks highly of
his sister, Marie, and is astonished
at Wicks' brilliantly astute
suggestion that maybe Marie is
trying to replace him as the star of
the family.

Woman: Equality

To be or not to be?

Can woman ever be the
equal of man?
Not without help.
Help from whom?
Man!
Men can help women who
are determined to take
man's role as natural
leaders of the Universe.

It's time that man took a rest.
For the first time in the history of the world,
man has the opportunity to live the good life.
A paradise, known only to woman, is about to be up
for grabs. The happy role of housewife is about to
be taken over by man.
Can he handle it? There's nothing to it.
Just lay back and whistle.

The New Homemaker

With woman safely stored at the office,
man's problems are over.
A few spoons of pablum,
a couple of dry diapers,
and it's back to the
T.V. set for the daily
"soaps."
"Home is boring,"
says woman.
Nonsense!
"Housework is a drag,"
says woman.
Rubbish!
Housework is fun
if it's done
in a fun way.

TURBAN

ASH

HAPPY HOUSE=
HUSBAND

Around the House

Vacuuming.
One of the easiest of jobs.
Plug in and push it
around the house.
The vacuum does the rest.
Don't move things like
furniture, beds
and tables.
What's the point?
By the time the working
wife gets home,
she'll be too exhausted to
notice the pieces that **are** showing.

WRONG   RIGHT

So why worry about the pieces that are not?

Stains and Marks

With the amount of sitting and
drinking that the newly
enrolled househusband will
be doing, accidents will
be inevitable.
Most spills can be
soaked up with a
paper towel.
On kitchen tile,
use a wet cloth.
On wooden floors,
a dry cloth.
And on all carpeted
areas, rearrange
the furniture.

Cooking

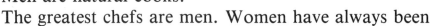

For the man who now
finds himself in the
fortunate position of
househusband, cooking
will be the job that
will present the least difficulty.
Men are natural cooks.
The greatest chefs are men. Women have always been
incredibly inept at cooking.
Those that have occasionally
presented an edible meal
have no doubt taken the
recipe from a book written
by a man.

So what advice can I give?
Do what comes naturally.
Whichever way it turns out
will be an improvement on
most meals served to working
men in the past.

This is not to say that the new
househusband has nothing to
learn from the ex-housewife.
He has.
He can learn to prepare the
most common meal served
by wives in the past. Stew.
It remains one of the least
appetizing meals that can be
presented to anyone who has
completed eight hours of hell
in a factory.

But – and here is the important
part – a stew is the easiest of
meals to prepare. Hence its
popularity by housewives of
yesterday.
So, what do we give the little
lady on a Monday (her most
exhausting day)?
Right on.
STEW.
Grab anything that comes
to mind.
Throw it in a large pot.
Bring to a boil and
leave on the stove
from two to six hours.
Serve hot to everyone but
yourself.
You are on a diet and are
too tired to eat after
slaving over a hot stove
all day.

Washing Dishes

Get a rhythm going.
A wonderful little song to pass
the time as you sink your hands
into the suds is the great Beatles
number "Yesterday."
So let's begin.

"I take a plate,
When I've washed it I will bake a cake.
Now I'll put it in the rack and take,
A knife and fork that will not break."
"Why did I wash it fast?
I don't know it didn't stay.
Now I'll dry a cup as I long
for one more plate to wash up,
One more plate. . . ."

And so on.

Who said working in the
kitchen wasn't fun?

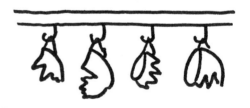

Making Beds

Does the bed really need
remaking? Many people are light
sleepers who toss and turn all night.
Others are out like a light
in the time it takes most people
to throw off their trousers.
Whichever sleeper has been in the
bed you're about to fix, there is
one golden rule.
Stripping is a no, no.
The moment clothes are removed
from the bed, they must be
returned to the same bed.
With the kettle whistling in
the kitchen you'll be faced
with all manner of boring items
to take care of, i.e., tucking in sheets,
folding under covers, fluffing up pillows.

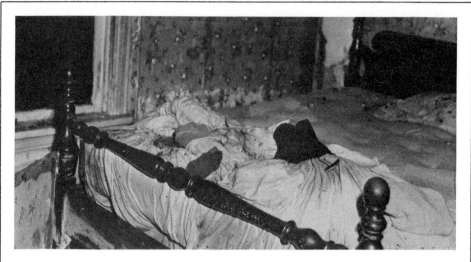

This beautifully unmade bed won the Importante Ricordare Conservare il Loro prize at a recent showing of househusbands' work in Venice. "I call it 'Sunshine Beauty' " said the modest Bert White of Sheffield, England. Note the simple breezy style given by easy-going free creases pulled taut to resemble a Cremona sunset.

There's no doubt about it.
Whatever you do, try not to
remove anything from the bed.
Grip the corners of the top sheet
nearest the pillow and tug.
Now fold back.
Most of the creases should be gone.   PILLOW
Those creases that do remain will disappear once you've
sat on them to wind the alarm for you wife's 6.00 AM call.

UNMADE

MADE

Many years of preparation were needed before the masterful Wicks plan could be completed. During the early stages the resourceful author was anxious that the world leaders be the first to know that such a plan was being prepared. Wicks first stop was the White House and a meeting with the late President of the United States of America.

Then off to Canada. And a meeting in Ottawa with Prime Minister Trudeau.

And finally. Mexico City where, although President Lopez Portillo appeared to like the idea. his guard did not.

75

Dusting

Dust is a dirt that collects
in unseen places.
Picture tops,
high shelves
and unread books
to name a few.
Dust out-of-sight is
dust out-of-mind.

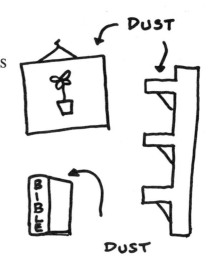

If the wife complains,
too bad.
You'll have to do something
about the problem.
First you'll need a stepladder.
A word of warning.
Ladders can be dangerous.
When holding it be careful
that your wife doesn't
fall on you.

Shopping for Food

Although all consumers will advise
you to make out a shopping list
before shopping, this is not
a good idea.
Who wants to sit in the house
making out shopping lists
when there's T.V. to watch?

Take a shopping cart as you enter
the store and head for your
first stop . . . the coffee counter.

There's a good chance
you'll meet a friend
or a neighbour.
Whatever happens,
sit down.
You are about
to start walking
and you may
as well rest
while you can.
Take one aisle
at a time.

It's a good idea to start
with meat.
Although it's expensive,
it's easy to grab and throw
in the cart.
Stop for coffee
at the end of each aisle.
There's no hurry.
You have hours to
stroll and hum.
The quiet music being
relayed over the speakers is
quite soothing and if the food
does cost a little more than
you counted on, who cares?
It's only money and, let's face it,
you're now the "little man" of the
house.
You don't have to go out to work
to get it.

Colonel Saunders listens intently as the patient, yet firm author outlines his plan for women colonels in the world of fast foods.

Ironing

Certainly one of the least
desirable of chores around
the house. For this very
reason it's a job that should
be completed as soon as possible.
First, sort the bundles of clothes
that you've taken from the dryer.
Place them in two piles.

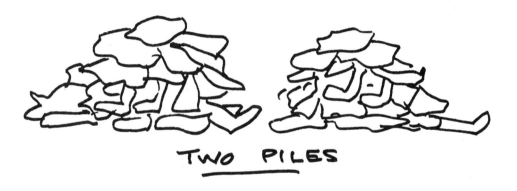

TWO PILES

Those that can be seen when worn and those that can't.
You are now ready to begin ironing.
Shirts are visible in the front, so don't worry
about the backs or sleeves.
Items never seen outside the house?
You got it . . . all non-ironed.
Nightgowns, sheets, socks, pillowcases. . . .
Who's going to see them, right?
Another household chore completed in record time
with man's natural ingenuity for planning.

Cleaning Windows

This will now be a job for the newly liberated woman. However, if you feel like putting on a show, then by all means grab a bottle of Windex and get started.

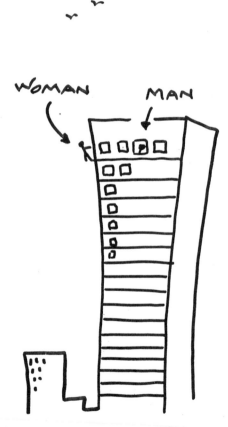

Is it a hard job? Not if you follow one simple rule. Always leave the outside for your exhausted working partner. It's by far the most difficult to clean. Especially if you happen to live on the seventy-eighth floor of an apartment block.

But this is not
your concern.
This is the
concern of the
new, weary,
breadwinner in
the house.
When is the
best time to
do the job?
A Saturday
morning, or
any time that
previous
arrangements
have been made
for a game of
golf with the
girls.

As to the cleaning itself – squirt the liquid onto
the glass and wipe off. Don't worry about the corners.
You can always suggest that this is dirt that is on
the outside . . . her side.

This beautifully cleaned window was washed by a new househusband, Frank Tonkin (as in Tonkin incident), of Chicago. "It was me first time ever, cross me heart," said the proud Frank during a recent television interview.

If they look the same when you finish as they did
when you started, pull the drapes.
How then will your mate know whether or not you've
cleaned the windows?
She won't.
But it's another good topic at the
supper table during a lull in the
conversation.
"I did the windows today.
I was fed up waiting for you
to get at them."

Knitting

The term knitting comes from the Anglo-Saxon word "cnyttan" which means to tie or knot.

It's a wonderfully appropriate name.

The boring application of this pastime can tie you up for hours.

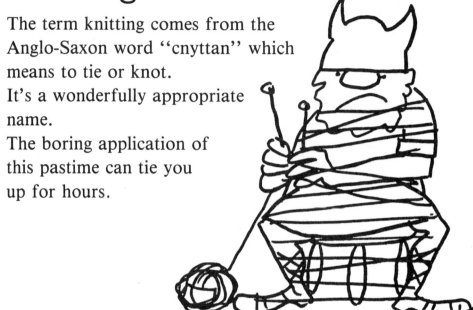

If you **must** knit, wait until your partner has sat down, comfortably watching T.V.

CLICK

CLICK

SQEAK

SQEAK

Michael Caine assured Wicks that the immensely attractive author was wasting his time trying to persuade Caine to give it all up and become a househusband.

Have the sound turned down (you wish to listen for the baby). Now reach for your knitting. There are two long needles that when banged together make an incredibly irritating, clicking noise. Get clicking. If you have a squeaky rocker, so much the better.

HAND KNITTED SWEATER

FACTORY KNITTED SWEATER

Sewing

A kindergarten game that can be lots of fun.
Find a small corner of the house and hide.
Grab some material and push it into
a sewing machine.
By turning the material
all manner of pretty
designs can be made on the
cloth.
Flowers and flowers and
flowers . . . and flowers.
As a change you may
occasionally make a dress.
Unfortunately these are never
to your liking, and will result
in your going to a store to
buy the finished article at
half the price that you
paid for the material
you originally bought.
Not to worry.
All is not lost.
The material makes first-class
dusting cloths.

Sewing on Buttons

These must be attached to the
clothing in such a way that it
will be impossible for them to
fall off before your partner
is safely out of the house.
Thread and needle are used.
This is forced through the
cloth and pulled tight.
The thread is then twisted
around the button.
This should hold the button
in place for an hour,
with luck.

I have heard of buttons being sewn
on cloth and staying there for days.
These were sewn on by people who
tied knots on the thread when
finishing the sewing.
However, these were creatures
of a bygone age.

WRONG

Attending Sales

Get there early.
Line up for hours.
Scramble, kick and
fight your way to a
piece of clothing that
you particularly like.

Then return home with
something you liked
better from the expensive store next door.

Buying a New Suit

Take your time.
Sit your partner down by the
changing room and glare at her
if she as much as looks at
another man. Although the shop
is filled with every style of
garment known to exist, make the
remark that there doesn't seem
to be anything in your size.
Try on as many suits as you can.
Show the more expensive ones to your bored partner.
MAKE SURE THAT SHE SEES THE PRICE TAG.

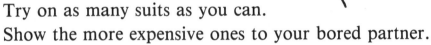

I COULD
WEAR
IT BOWLING

"It's not for you. It makes you
look big," she will lie.
Now parade in an exorbitantly
expensive suit – though not as
expensive as the suit that you saw
when you first entered the store.
Your relieved partner will throw
her charge-card at you before you
can change your mind.
"Thank you dear. Don't you just
love it?" you'll say as you leave
the store with a smile.

Clothes

You do not have any!
Regardless of a closet so full that you've taken space in your partner's closet, you still do not have

anything to wear. What does this mean? It means that the suit that you bought last week is no longer the right size, and worse, is completely out of fashion. On the other hand: your partner with one dress, two pairs of jeans and a pair of coveralls, is equipped to sip tea with the Queen at Buckingham Palace.

YOU

YOUR PARTNER

The Telephone

Once an instrument of torture, now an absolute necessity.
How else will your neighbour across the street know that
the coffee is ready?

I WAS JUST CALLING YOU!

Those incredible reasons
for phoning are now yours.
"How about a game of tennis?"
"Guess who just split?"
"Did you hear the latest about...?"
By the time your partner is
back from a hard day at the
office, you've had more
calls than a telephone operator.

One thing to remember.
If the phone rings in the evening and it's for the children,
get them off quick.
There's no sense in wearing out the instrument!

*The dedicated author travelled to the home of Minnesota
Fats to outline his plan to get men back into the homes
and women out to work. "But I work at home!" said the
great player, before taking Wicks' shirt, tie, scarf, hat,
gloves, shoes and socks in a friendly game of pool.*

Suggested Jobs (Non-Paying)

Flag days: Pick a day,
any day, and hold
a tray of flags.
To alleviate the boredom,
rattle a small can toward
the people who are hurrying
past on the street.

Collecting for Symphony Orchestras: Get together with as many
unmusical people as you
can and discuss ways of
taking money from people
who are even less interested
in music than any of your
group.

Worthwhile Charities: Any that refuse to pay wages
regardless of the amount of
time spent collecting.

Charity Work

If for some incredible reason you
occasionally feel like getting out
of the house, be certain that you are not
involved in work that will result in payment.

It's true that such payment could help defray
the costs of running the home, but it's also true that
such an action would take away the sense of
superiority that the newly liberated woman
has fought so hard to get!
Remember, she's out there slaving for **you**.
Don't take away her fun.

Door Callers

Answer the door yourself.
It may be for charity.
If the old, mean, bread
winner gets to the door
first, the caller will
be lucky to get a
slice of dry bread.

Before giving ten
dollars you may ask
what the charity is
in aid of; though
this isn't important.

What is important is
that your exhausted partner,
laid out in the front room
reading the evening paper,
reaches for the ten bucks.

She may scowl, but it's you who
will get the thanks and the smile as you
hand over the money to the charity worker at the door.

Holidays

As the new househusband you are now in a position to dictate where everyone will be spending their holidays.
It's important to be aware that your wife now has only three weeks' holiday a year from the noise and bustle of the factory.
What she needs is complete rest.
Lots of peace and quiet.
Birds, flowers, bees, gentle breezes, the bending and swaying of hay about to be mown.

AFRICA

What she needs is Disneyland.

As the newly liberated working person,
your wife will be taking the children on all the rides;
and carrying the children everywhere
when they are too tired to walk.
All the driving will now be done by your wife
(the traffic is much too busy for you).
Meantime you will be free to look at all the shops
as you slowly edge your way through the heavy traffic.

Pay careful attention – these are the shops you can
return to when you're out looking
for the much-needed souvenirs for
your side of the family back home.

The ideal spot to relax and enjoy a holiday beside the sea.

By the time you finally reach your motel room with the children, the only place open will be a disco and an expensive restaurant. Look out of the window. See? It's too dark to play golf, even if she did feel energetic enough to play.

Another great spot for a holiday!

Yet another.

After the trip you should be broke.
The working woman will remark,
"Well, it was a great holiday."
To which you reply,
"It sure was. Though not as nice
as last year's."

More . . .

. . . great . . .

. . . spots.

The Silent Treatment

Having had a fun-filled day, it's quite possible that home will suddenly appear boring to you, once your mate returns from the factory. This is natural. You have been with friends all day, playing tennis, or watching quiz shows.

THEN THE BOSS SAID...

BOR..ING!

Whoever the people are that you have seen throughout the day they all have one thing in common.
All are happy, fresh and attractive.

Now this tired sack of potatoes crosses your threshold.
Be careful.
Given the opportunity, this worn-out piece of refuge will try to tell you about an office happening or a promotion that's heading her way.

Whatever the story, none will
equal day-time television.
Stop the story
as quickly as
possible.
This will involve a
sullen stare and a
tightening of the lips.

TIGHT LIPS

SULLEN

Some partners can adopt this stance for
weeks or even months.
I suggest one week.

FORGIVE
ME. IT
WAS MY
FAULT,
I
THINK!

When to stop?
When the following
line is heard.
"I can't stand this
silence. Say something!
Anything!"
To which you reply.
"You really don't
know what's wrong, do you?"

In no time at all your partner will be begging forgiveness
for whatever it is she thinks she may have done to
deserve the "silent treatment."

Exercising

Years of hanging around the
house walloping down candies
have given most women the
shapes of pregnant whales.

Now man will be at home.
This cannot happen and
must not happen to him!
The body of man has
been honed and shaped
over a million years.
God would never forgive us
if we allowed this perfection to
go the way of most housewives.
What can man do to avert this
hideous happening?

Exercise.
Where?
There are two places.
Out of the home and inside the home.
Let's look at the first.

Women's Health Clubs

Over the years money-hungry beings,
sensing the need for women to acquire
a shape acceptable to man,
have opened health clubs.
A small disused building
is filled with various pieces
of equipment.
As the money rolls in the
exercise equipment is rolled
back to be replaced by equipment
that does little to a shape,
except expand on the original.
Coffee bars, snack bars and
bar-bars have lept between the
stationary bicycles and swept them into dark corners.
Today's woman joining a health club is hurried through
the gym to be shown the impressive bar where she and
her friends can while away their days in a series of merry
arm-bend exercises.

Men's Health Clubs

The same as above.
If your working partner
will foot the bill,
you could spend many
a happy hour there.
And you can always
use the pool. . . .

*An instructor at a typical women's
health club is shocked by the
suggestion of a new member
that the class do some exercise.*

Exercising in the Home

Many feel that this section is now going
to be devoted to throwing
our bodies all over the house.
Nothing could be further from the
truth.
We are not going to act like madmen
in order to lose a few pounds.

We are going to act
like normal healthy
members of the human
race and enjoy ourselves
as we roll back the
unwelcome fat.

How?
By having sex.

Making love three times a week will enable
us to lose more than four pounds a month.
And although there are faster ways of
taking off the weight – there's not a more fun way.

"By making love you
lose weight without the
use of dieting, exercise
machines or weight pills"
says Dr. Abraham Friedman,
who has worked exclusively
on weight control for the
past twenty-six years.

HI THERE
SAILOR

Dr. Friedman found that
many of his overweight
patients had sexual
problems.
"They were substituting
food for sex," he said.
Then why not reverse the
procedure and use sex
in the place of food?

Sexual intercourse doubles
the pulse rate up to 150
a minute.
This causes many of the muscles
to contract and expends about
200 calories during an average
sex act.

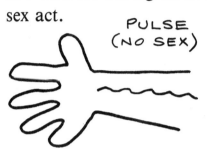

PULSE
(NO SEX)

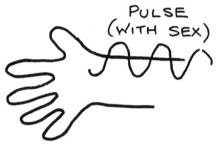

PULSE
(WITH SEX)

Let's look at the many
overweight people who
have a bedtime snack of
say, a piece of pie and
a glass of milk.

Gain in calories: 700.

By substituting sex for
the snack they could save
900 calories.
For every three times
they get into the sack,
they lose a pound.
(This is on the
basis of 2,400
calories to every
pound of body
weight.)

What if a person is still hungry after sex?
"You have not been doing your
post coital afterplay," says
the doctor.
So there it is men.
Straight from the expert's mouth.

I know that the afterplay can be a shocking bore
but if man is to keep his shape then he must
make sacrifices.
So when you've finished exercising don't say
"Well that's that. Good night," and turn over.
Hang in there and have a cuddle.
Even if you don't feel like it, remember –
you owe it to yourself to preserve your God-given body.

PART THREE

Despite the wonderful way the plan to liberate women is taking shape, many men will feel that they are unable to take full advantage of *any* scheme to get women out into the workforce and men back into the home.

These will be the single men.

Men who, for whatever reason, have never had (or hoped to have) a woman to carry out their every wish.

They feel, quite rightly, that there is not much point in staying home to watch the "soaps," if you haven't got a partner slaving out there in the concrete jungle bringing home the bacon.

Obviously these men will need to know how they can get a working girl of their very own.

Women:
How To Get One

The first thing to remember is that man has
a master advantage in the game known as
"getting a piece of the other."
He is a man and every woman wants one.
Many will feel this statement hard to believe.
These will be the men who
have been unable to get close enough
to a woman to persuade her to do anything other
than take his coat at a cloakroom.
Not only are these men unmarried,
but many are living alone, or with
another man.
Whichever you are, remember . . .
"YOU ARE A MAN AND EVERY WOMAN WANTS ONE."

Getting One
On a Train

Board a crowded train.
Make your way to the nearest
woman who takes your fancy.
Get beside her and if you're tall
enough, grab a strap. (Not a part
of her . . . a part of the train).
Carry a newspaper and begin to read.
This action will immediately separate
you from the usual creeps who attempt
to push themselves against women on crowded trains.

Which kind of newspaper?
The New York Times is perfect.
It's never interesting enough
to encourage others to look
over your shoulder, plus
the pages are large enough
to cover even the most
disgusting of acts, should
your conduct get completely
out of control.

As the train leaves the station throw your body
against hers.
She will give a quiver.
Say "I'm terribly sorry," in as low a voice as
you can muster considering the circumstances.
"Be my guest," she will answer.
Fold your newspaper over her head and, as the train
jerks once more, cushion your lips against hers.
Before the train is in the tunnel she'll be in
your arms.
You have made a prisoner of love.
But more important, you have a prisoner of labour.
Another female has "bit the dust" as she rides
toward equality.

Getting One
On a Plane

Remember:

YOU ARE A MAN AND EVERY WOMAN WANTS ONE.
On a plane, time is of the utmost importance.
Don't wait two hours to spring your trap if
the duration of the flight is ninety minutes.

Let's be honest.
Despite our motto "... every woman wants one" there
are better places to try the theory than on a plane.
For one thing the competition is ridiculous.
Of the 200 passengers on the average
aircraft, four or five at the most will be women.
The chance of one of them sitting next to you
is remote to say the least.
If you insist on "making it" as you fly, then
you'd better take aim at a stewardess.

She is by far the easiest of women
to trap into a life of drudgery.
Most of them have taken the job in the
hopes of snaring anything in long
trousers that smokes a pipe.

Success depends on
the following
important step –

ECONOMY

Make sure that you are
travelling first class.
In one fell swoop
you've eliminated
199 peasants and
have now joined three
men in their eighties,
two women in their
seventies and a pilot
with a free pass.
You are now
the Robert Redford
of the airways.

FIRST

Settle back and ask the stewardess for the Wall Street Journal.
This is not a bricklayer's magazine but is in fact the businessman's bible in making a sackful of the green stuff.

Then tell the stewardess that it's your first flight on a regular aircraft. Your private jet has a flat tire. Mention how wonderful it is to travel with the peasants and how fascinated you are at seeing how the other half lives from close hand.

However you decide to follow up this statement, your words will fall on deaf ears. She's already plotting how to drop the name of her hotel and is ready for gathering in. Your restful days as a househusband can be enjoyed in the quiet of your pad as the little lady continues to cry her wares "Coffeee, Tea or Milk" a million miles from your sweet-smelling cigar and hard liquor.

Getting One
If You're Short

Many men find their lack of height an added burden when seeking female company.

I say to these men that the world is full of little guys who have really turned on women.

Hitler, Napoleon and Dick Cavett to name a few.

What is it that they have that tall men do not?

They have the ability to steer women away from their shortcomings.

A hidden talent?

In a way.

A more accurate description would be a hidden weapon.

Many women are convinced that a man short in height has been endowed with extra length in a completely different area of his anatomy.

Shorty Kohnson of Kansas City grabs for an attractive girl's hand in order to show her his most pleasing feature.

Getting That Little Extra

Any short man, fair, dark, fat
or ugly can acquire what woman
desires.
Various contraptions
are on the market.
I myself would
recommend
the weight and pull
method.

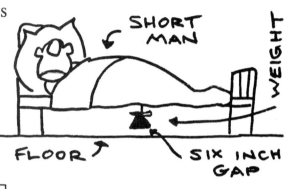

A small weight is tied
to the end of the object
in question before sleep
and dangled from the bed.
(the weight should hang
about six inches from the
floor and is increased in
size every three days.)
Begin with three ounces,
slowly increasing the weight
to around a five-pound maximum.
When the weight finally touches
the ground you have attained an
inducement that any working
woman will be proud to run
home to.

*A male model is seen
here demonstrating a
five-pound weight
during a recent medical
exhibition.*

When To
Get One

Mark it down. June the 22nd.
It's the most important date
in the history of man. Why?
Because, men, June the 22nd is the day
that they're biting.
I should say jumping, grabbing, clawing.
It's the one day in the year when all things
come together for a woman.
Physically, mentally, anxiously
she needs, wants and craves a man.

*A group of sex-craved women steal up on the
unwary Frank Brown of Calgary as he sits with
his mother enjoying a June 22nd picnic.*

Doctor David Reuben in his book *Any Woman Can!*
tells us just the time for our single male to
chase and capture his future working mate.
"She is most receptive sexually each month
just before ovulation," says Doctor Reuben.
"However, her sexual feelings intensify
dramatically during warm weather since the
pineal gland is attuned to the long summer
hours of sunlight.
No one knows exactly why, but among human beings
conception (and incidentally marriage) seems to reach
its peak around June twenty-second, the longest day
of the year."*

JUNE 21ST   JUNE 22ND

*David Reuben, *Any Woman Can!* (New York: David McKay
Company, Inc., 1971), p. 89.

Doctor Reuben goes on to suggest that the reason is rooted in man's primitive past. That infants conceived at this time will be born about April the 1st of the following year, giving the child a full six months to grow strong before the cold weather sets in.

Woman may be more willing to be taken on June 22nd . . . but the facts show that woman is ALWAYS willing to be taken by man.
Ready to work.
Ready to slave.
And not just in the home.

Woman now wants to join the tension-driving madhouse outside the home.
And not just for a day.
Woman wants responsibility.
Woman wants man's work.
Woman wants a shot at equality.
Woman should get it.

MAN DESERVES IT!

Woman:
And the Act of Sex

Since we have resolved the problem of how and when to get a woman, it only remains for us to look at what a man should do with a woman once he has one.

Although man, the intellectual, is quite happy to talk when out with a woman, most women are not listening.

Man, the talker, is a far different creature from man, the doer. And woman knows it.

INTELLIGENT TALK

COMIC

Man may know the answer to a balance-of-payment problem, but give him the task of unfastening a brassiere in the dark alley and man has more fingers and thumbs than a disjointed octopus.

In the world of sex, woman is the master.

For this reason I have decided to give a short basic guide to the act of sex.

Long before you get cracking in the sex department, it's important that a certain number of actions take place. These actions are known as "foreplay."
Instructions are given for variations of the more common action.

Kissing

– also known as bussing.

Although women go absolutely bananas over this particular action, most men would happily prefer to dispense with this "*hors d' oeuvre*" and get cracking on the entree.

BEFORE

AFTER

Let's begin with the basic action. The lips of both parties are pressed together. That's it! Nothing more. Nothing less. Most women want it with the mouth open. Having cleaned their teeth and squirted their mouths with all kinds of junk, they certainly don't want their expensive breaths to go to waste. . .

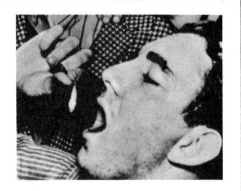

A kissing beginner wisely practises on a fish.
Note the interesting open-mouth technique.

The French Kiss

Both parties open their mouths and after first making sure that the lips are touching (poking the tongue out without first touching the lips can be disastrous), the tongues then feel their way around the inside of the partner's mouth until such time as the partner's tongue is found.

Both parties then touch tongue tips.

I know it sounds bloody revolting, but all I can do is present the facts.

The dangers of French Kissing are vividly shown in this rare picture of a class in action at a South West Paris finishing school for lovemakers. A careless pupil is seen dead on the floor having sucked when he should have blown. His tongue has wrapped itself around his trachia causing instant strangulation.

Eyelid Kissing

As the word suggests.
One of the partners places
his or her lips against
the other's eyelid.
For both partners to do
this at the same time
will require one of them
to be upside down.
The other important factor?
One eyelid at a time is kissed.

Aghast at the suggestive kiss he has just received from his fiancee, a young and eager man demonstrates the kind of "safe" kiss he had in mind. The receiver is the gentle and kind father of the bride to be.

Love Bites

A form of kissing.
One partner decides to
give the lips of the other
a miss, and aims for the
neck. He or she takes a
piece of flesh in his or
her mouth and delivers
a sucking action.
This results in the
recipient bearing the
mark of a sore that
resembles a cross between
leprosy and a bad fried egg.
This kind of kissing is usually carried out by the young.
They feel that to leave such a mark proves that
"they were there."

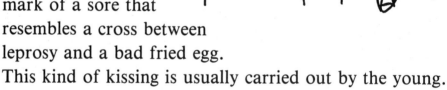

By the way . . .
as a wrapup to these instructions on kissing, all
breathing is conducted through the nose.

Woman: Sex With

Positions:
Two.
Standing and *Lying*.

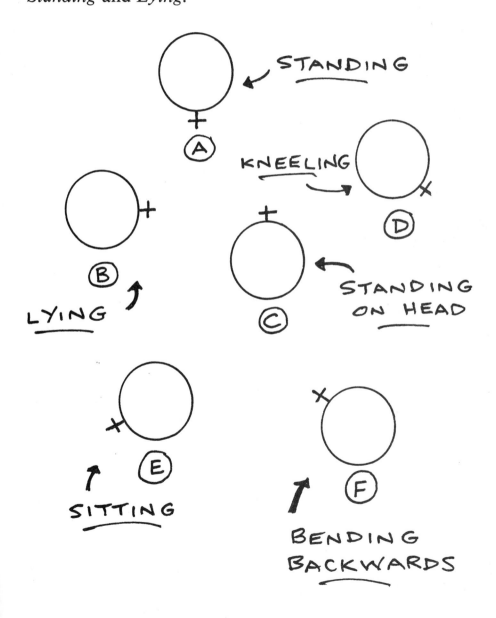

STANDING

(A)

KNEELING

(D)

(B)

LYING

STANDING
ON HEAD

(C)

(E)

SITTING

(F)

BENDING
BACKWARDS

Standing

Place the woman against the nearest wall (no sense in falling down during the exercise) You are now ready to begin to have sex. A woman can close her eyes and imagine that her partner is Robert Redford (with the exception of your face, all other parts of a normal man should be equal).

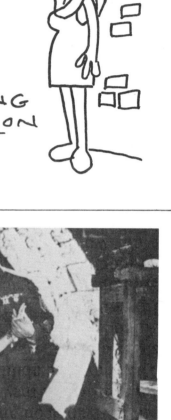

STARTING POSITION

Anxious to get involved in the standing position, two lively men argue as to whose wall is the closest.

Unfortunately man does not have the same advantage.
His eyes can be shut tighter than a clamshell
but even the thickest of idiots will know that
the party he is pressed
against is not Raquel Welch.
Can this problem be eliminated?
Partly.

READY WHEN YOU ARE!

Before beginning the act of sex,
throw the dress of the would-
be recipient over her head.
This covering-up solves one
of two problems common with men.

GUESS WHO?

Non Erection: Man can pretend
that the figure
under the dress
is in fact Raquel
Welch.

Premature
Ejaculation: Man can pretend
that the figure
under the dress
is his favourite
hockey star.

Lying

Both parties lower themselves to the floor.
Both parties press their backs to the ground.
The man takes the right hand of his partner
in his left hand. (A)

Reach over with right hand and take partner's
left hand (B)

Pull hard and . . . (C)?
So endeth the first lesson.
(What did you expect for the price of this book?)

You are now involved in the art of sex!
Sure it's not what it's cracked up to be,
but what the hell. Women
want it and who is
man to argue?
However there is a
slight problem.
Our plan to encourage
women to get what
they want, namely
out of the home
and into the
workforce, can hit
a rock with the
introduction of intercourse.

The fact that you are beaming
and woman is giggling does
not necessarily mean that
everything in the garden is
as it should be.

Once you have left this being
against the wall and have taken
a cab home, other forces can
come into play.

Forces so potent that the very word causes men of every
race and creed to cringe in dark corners.
The word? . . . . . . PREGNANCY.

Woman: The Pregnant One

The words "I'm pregnant" have turned the bravest of men throughout the centuries into blobs of jelly.
Today is no exception.
Regardless of how successful our plan is to have woman up to her arms in axle grease, a bun in the oven will have her sinking back into man's favourite chair faster than man can say "It couldn't be me. I was out of town all last month."

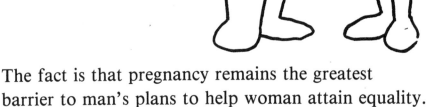

MAYBE IT'S SOMETHING YOU ATE!

The fact is that pregnancy remains the greatest barrier to man's plans to help woman attain equality.

PREGNANT WOMEN WILL NOT WORK.

Women throughout the centuries have constantly leaned on the ailment known as pregnancy as an excuse to gain sympathy, seats on the subway or an all-round easy life as the man of the house doubles his workload.

If woman is to gain her full independence and so leave man to have his turn at the good life, then woman must remain childless.

To this end, it's as well to review why a woman's tum suddenly balloons, forcing her to drop everything and flop around the house like a washed-up porpoise.

The Inside Story

Man has a sperm "A."
Woman has an egg "B."
"A" must meet "B" or it's
"Goodbye Charlie."
Let's follow a typical
uncontrolled man who has
suddenly found his private
part trapped inside that
particular part of a woman.
"A" has been released and
now finds himself in a strange
neighbourhood. "B' has just
left her ovary and is off for a
stroll downtown.
Hearing "A" approaching,
"B" jumps immediately into a
fallopian alley and lies in wait.
She then leaps onto "A"
forcing him to the ground.
Finding it impossible to escape
from under "B," "A" begins
to burrow into "B."
The damage is done.
The sound of tiny feet are on
their way.
Man is once again about to
take his place at the factory
gates leaving woman to enjoy
life at home.

Woman: And The Pill

If pregnancy is woman's number one barrier to equality

then surely sex cannot be far behind.
Woman's insatiable lust for man's attentions has
invariably driven her headlong toward intercourse.

Does this mean that women must choose between
sex and equality?
Not at all.
Women can have both.

Woman can continue to enjoy the warmth and closeness of the vibrant animal known as man.
A simple pill allows it.

The Pill: How It Works

Shaped like any other pill THE pill is swallowed just before intercourse.

"THE" PILL   OTHER PILLS

Once in the mouth it quickly heads for the fallopian tube.
Here it lies in wait, looking down from a great height on the egg that is anxiously waiting the arrival of the first sperm.

PILL

PILL LYING IN WAIT

EGG

Suddenly the sperm arrives and begins to
make its way toward the waiting egg.
Before the egg and sperm can come into
contact, the pill makes its move.

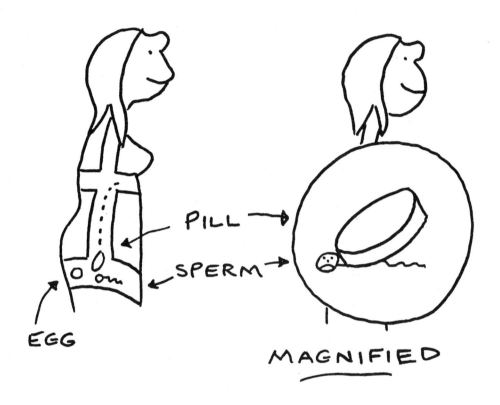

PILL →

SPERM →

EGG

MAGNIFIED

Down it comes, crushing the poor
unsuspecting sperm beneath its weight.
Another of God's creatures has gone the way
of all things.

Woman is free to continue her fight and man
can relax again, safe in the knowledge that his
plan for early retirement is continuing on its
merry way.

When to Take
The Pill

Whenever.
Wherever.
However: Never take the
pill in the presence of a man.

To do this suggests that
the woman is an "easy lay."
Bang will go all the free gifts.
Out will go all the free meals.
Away will go all the free movies.

HI THERE.
I'M ON THE PILL!

All the acts of bribery
that man had thought necessary to get a girl
into the sack, will go straight out the window.

No more, "What kind of a girl do you think I am?"
No more, "I never do it on a first date,"
and certainly no more of, "tell me you love me,
then you can."

Is there another way?
There is not!
"So what about vasectomy?" you say.
What about it?
This incredibly brutal act which has been perpetrated
by women in recent years, has found
many men falling under the knife.
If God had wanted man to have
part of his magnificent body
disfigured, he would have built
man with the shape of
the average woman.

Besides, who are we to attack
the tool of life?
Vasectomy is out.
The Pill is in. So there.

But for some it is already too late.
These poor souls have exposed their private parts
to a scissors-carrying fiend in a surgeon's gown.
This must stop.
But is it possible?
Never fear, Wicks is here.
Many will say that once vasectomised
always vasectomised.
Rubbish!
This myth spread by women to avoid
their pill-taking duty
does not wash worth a damn.
Man can be man again . . . I should know.

Vasectomy

Some years ago I seriously considered having a vasectomy. A fellow journalist gave me the idea as I stood drinking coffee in the corner of the newsroom.

"It's the greatest thing since the first apple."

I asked him to lower his voice and steered him towards a quiet corner.

"E'Er, does it hurt?" I asked.

"Hurt? Of course it doesn't hurt."

This poor sod was photographed leaving the operating theatre after his vasectomy operation.

"But I thought they had to cut something."
"So does a barber."
'How long does it take?"
"Twenty minutes!"
"Twenty minutes! Are you sure?"
"Of course I'm sure,
though I did hear of one
guy who did it in five
minutes, but that was in China."

NEXT!

"Er, isn't there a pill a guy can take?"
"It won't work. It's this . . .," he made a quick
movement across his throat with his finger,
"or nothing."

I dialed the number of the doctor.
Why is it that whenever a man wants to
discuss a delicate matter with a doctor
it's a woman who always answers the phone?

"I'd like to speak to the doctor please."
"Name?"
"Wicks."
"What do you wish
to speak to the
doctor about, Mr. Wicks?"
"Er . . . a private matter."
"Medical?"
"Sort of."
"Do you have a pain?"
This was getting ridiculous.
I took a deep breath.
"I'd like an acupuncture . . . I mean I'd like a . . .!"
Good grief.
I'd forgotten the name of the operation.
"Is it internal?" she asked.
"No!"

"Is it in your head?"

"No!"

"Your stomach?"

"Getting warm. . . ."

"Mr Wicks. We're very busy and I wonder if you wouldn't mind. . . ."

"It's my private parts," I blurted out.

"You want a vasectomy?"

"Er . . . yes please."

"There's a rather long waiting list."

"How long?"

"Ten weeks."

I told my wife the news.

"It could have been worse," she said.

"Like what?"

"Like nine months."

"Very funny." I was in no mood for laughing.

"Why not ring your own doctor?"

"Are you mad, woman. Someone we know?"

She finally persuaded me and I phoned.

"We do have a doctor in our building who has started in that very field."

I was shocked.

"A beginner? I mean it's not as if I was having a tooth out or getting a new pair of glasses."

HOW'S THE VASECTOMY?

"I assure you, Ben. This guy is one of the very best. He trained in England and is a surgeon."

The patient is ready for a vasectomy operation, doctor.

Convinced, I phoned this "Barnard" of
the vasectomy world and made an appointment.
The steps in the medical building led to
the lower floor. Obviously.
The smell of new paint filtered through
the walls as I made my way to
an empty waiting room.
I sat, picked up a magazine,
and waited.
A door opened, and a
receptionist entered.
"Mr. Wicks?"
I nodded.
"The doctor will
see you now."

He sat behind a
cluttered desk.
A small East
Indian man
in a white coat.

"Good evening,
Mr. Wicks,"
he said, using
a remarkable
impersonation
of Peter Sellers
impersonating
an East Indian.

AFTER

BEFORE

VASECTOMY

"Please take a seat.
I understand that you want
a vasectomy, is that so?"
"I do."
"Of course you understand
that we are very particular
whom we operate on."
"No. I didn't know that!"

CLOSE YOUR
EYES FOR A
BIG SURPRIZE!

For instance,
"I do not perform this
kind of operation on a
single chap."

IT'S OKAY. I'VE
HAD A VAS!

"I'm married."

"Happily?"

"Very!"

I looked at my watch.

Five minutes had gone.

If my friend was right about this lark,

it would be all over in

about fifteen minutes.

An apprehensive patient waits as a vasectomy specialist
and his assistant prepare for the difficult operation.

"I want you to fill
out this form. And do you
understand that when
I do this operation
there is no turning
back."
I had no intention of
turning back and told
him so.

"Maybe you do and
Maybe you don't. But
some doctors do a
temporary job. I don't!
Do you understand?"
"I do!"

TEMPORARY

For goodness sake!
Ten minutes to go.
maybe he's out to break the Chinese record.
I could kick myself.
That's what you get when you go to a "no
waiting" guy.

He suddenly stood and opened the door to a
small outer room.
"Would you please step in here, Mr Wicks."
I hurried in and stood by a couch covered by
a clean white sheet.

I looked at my watch.
Five minutes to go.
If this guy was going to
keep within the twenty-
minute time limit he was
going to need some help.
I unfastened my belt and was
about to remove my trousers as the
doctor entered the room.

"Please remove your shoes, Mr Wicks."
I stopped what I was doing.
"Remove my what?" I asked in amazement.
"Your shoes, Mr Wicks."
Had I heard right? I began to smile. My shoes . . .?
So that's why they have a population problem in
India!
I began to laugh . . . all those people running around
with no toes thinking they're protected . . . I couldn't
hold back and doubled over laughing.
The doctor's mouth dropped.
His face had taken on a look of sheer terror.
I tried to explain . . . of course he was worried about
my shoes spoiling his clean white sheet.
But it was too late for explanations . . . I was
laughing hysterically. . . .
Four-hundred-million people toeless . . . population
control gone mad . . . the tears were rolling down my
face as I staggered toward my car holding my beltless
trousers up with one hand and my side with the other.

The Vasectomy
Operation

But what if you've been fixed?
Is there any turning back?
Was the Indian doctor right?
Not in every case.
Many knots have been tied loosely enough to be
untied again.
But first we will need to look at the operation
The operation, naturally takes place on the lower half
of the body.
Taking the private part in his right hand the doctor,
along with the help of a qualified nurse, pulls.
When the private part is at the required length the
nurse immediately ties it off with a piece of string.
(Imagine a balloon that has been tied to hold in the
air and you will have some idea of the action.)

Now the doctor is ready to carry out the trickiest part of all.

Passing the end over and under (remembering the golden rule: left hand over and right hand under) a reef knot is tied in the stricken area.

REEF

TYING OFF

Man is now released into the world knowing that he is able to satisfy the many anxious women after his body; yet safe in the knowledge that he will never be forced to give up his life of ease for a pregnant factory worker.

Women:
The Holdouts

Unfortunately for exhausted man,
not all women **want** to be liberated.
Many feel that the braless mass stomping
the streets upset the quiet of their domain.
These women are the happy homemakers.
A group that must be persuaded to
join their sisters if man's plan
for early retirement is to work.

It's one thing for man to stay home with his newly
won freedom and it's quite another to find that he's
home with someone constantly reminding him that
there is work to be done around the house.

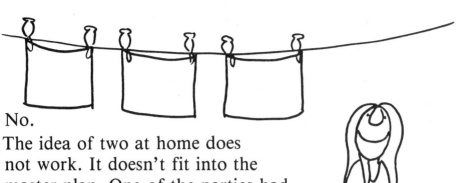

No.
The idea of two at home does not work. It doesn't fit into the master plan. One of the parties had better get out to work. And it had better be a she! But . . . can this happy little nappy-folder be made to leave the kitchen? It will not be easy. She feels that the marching martyr of the butch dress is not the kind of person on which the average woman wishes to build her future dreams.

If the woman's movement is to swell with these holdouts it had better shape up in the appearance department.

Most of these "libbers" look like the stragglers from a retreat to Moscow.

And it's not enough for them to start looking like women. . . .

They need to look like **more attractive** women THEN the stay-at-homers will want to join the bandwagon!

Having seen many feminists, I must admit that the task is neither a happy nor easy one.

Since time began women have made the effort to improve their appearance by the use of artificial aids. (Unlike man who, for obvious reasons, has never had to.)

Here, then, are a few tips for the many women who need them. All man has to do is to provide encouragement.

A typical Woman's Liberation Movement
leader takes time out for a little fishing.

Women: Cosmetics

Whatever a woman dislikes about her appearance can be fixed by slapping on the opposite of what lies underneath.

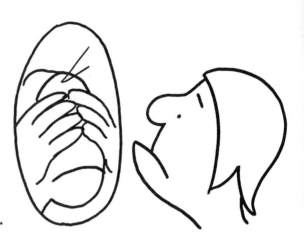

 Look a little white? Slap on some red.

 Mouth too small? Paint it big.

 Mouth too big? Paint it small.

 Got pimples? Cover them up.
Got oily skin? Clog the pores with powder.
Got dry skin? Clog the pores with oil.

Lets begin with the most important problem.

The face.

The biggest enemy?

Wrinkles!

Although these appear on
the surface of the skin,

it's under the skin that the culprit lies.

Muscles are the enemy.
As they roll all over the
place under the skin,

little waves constantly move under the surface.

Imagine a rock thrown into a puddle, and
you have some idea of what happens when
a woman opens her mouth.

The facial skin follows the muscles.

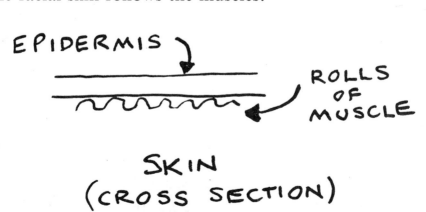

EPIDERMIS

ROLLS
OF
MUSCLE

SKIN
(CROSS SECTION)

More than one chin?
With the exception of a
good stiff toothbrush
pushed up under the
nose eighty-five
times a day,
most exercises
are a waste of time.

A large polo neck sweater is a surefire answer,
and if you itch when a piece of wool hits you
under the chin, then there is nothing else
for it. . . .
You've got it –
A FACE LIFT.

The Face Lift

Take the right hand
and place it at the back
of the head.
Grab a hunk of hair three
times a day and pull.
This should straighten
out the wrinkles in
the forehead.
Hold this position
for ten minutes, now release.
Unfortunately there are
a few side effects.

The nose will begin to creep
up the face along with the mouth.
Only you can decide
which you prefer.
Wrinkles in the forehead –
or a nose level with
your hairline.

BEFORE

AFTER

Crows' Feet

CROWS
FEET

These are lines that appear
around a woman's eyes.

They are caused mainly by
woman's insatiable appetite
for a man and is the result
of constant winking.

Cure:
Place the thumbs against
the bones beside the
eyes and press.

Warning:
This can be absolute hell
and will eventually
make a person cross-eyed.

But, I hasten to add,
cross-eyed without crow's feet!

AFTER

Women: What Now?

Many will feel that this book sets out to
show the ugly side of women.
It is true that the temptation to write
such a book was with me continually.
However, being a man, I was able to
overcome such prejudice.

**I am a strong believer in equality for women
and I hope that this book will speed the day
when women *themselves* will feel the equal of men.**

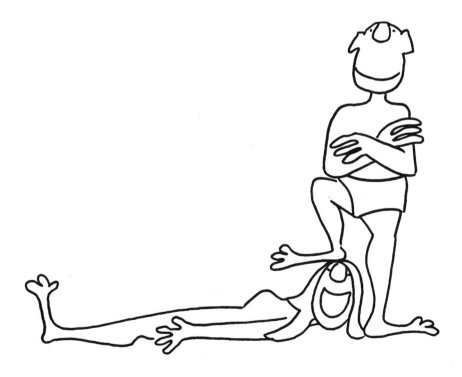